Health

How to Naturally Boost Your Immune System with Powerful Natural Methods and be Virtually Disease Proof!

Contents

Chapter 1. Why Improve Your Immune System. 1

Chapter 2. Natural Supplements that Work..... 5

Chapter 3. Herbal Teas for a Quick Boost 13

Chapter 4. Foods to Add in That Really Work .... .25

Chapter 5. Smoothie Recipes to Delight & Help 35

Chapter 6. Various Herbal Remedies as a Booster 50

Chapter 7. Immune Boosting Essential Oils .. 62

Chapter 8. Bonus Habits to Help.................... 68

© **Copyright 2019 by Robert S. Lee Publishing- All rights reserved.**

This document is geared toward providing exact and reliable information in regard to the topic and issue covered. The publication is sold with the idea that the publisher is not required to render accounting, officially permitted, or otherwise, qualified services. If advice is necessary, legal or professional, a practiced individual in the profession should be ordered.

- From a Declaration of Principles which was accepted and approved equally by a Committee of the American Bar Association and a Committee of Publishers and Associations.

In no way is it legal to reproduce, duplicate, or transmit any part of this document in either electronic means or in printed format. Recording of this publication is strictly prohibited and any storage of this document is not allowed unless with written permission from the publisher. All rights reserved.

The information provided herein is stated to be truthful and consistent, in that any liability, in terms of inattention or otherwise, by any usage or abuse of any policies, processes, or directions contained within is the solitary and utter responsibility of the recipient reader. Under no circumstances will any legal responsibility or blame be held against the publisher for any reparation, damages, or monetary loss due to the information herein, either directly or indirectly.

Respective authors own all copyrights not held by the publisher.

The information herein is offered for informational purposes solely, and is universal as so. The presentation of the information is without contract or any type of guarantee assurance.

The trademarks that are used are without any consent, and the publication of the trademark is without permission or backing by the trademark owner. All trademarks and brands within this book are for clarifying purposes only and are the owned by the owners themselves, not affiliated with this document.

Chapter 1. Why Improve Your Immune System

It's simple. The reason that your immune system is so important tis because it's what makes your body fight off sickness. It's what makes you feel healthy, and it protects your body from your cells to your organs, and it'll keep colds, flues, and ailments away, so it's important that you boost your immune system.

If you seem to be getting sickness after sickness, cold after cold, then you need to find a way to strengthen your immune system. It's important that you pay attention to your health, especially during and while preparing for cold and flu season. Your immune system has to work hard throughout the year, so it's important that it's strong enough to keep up with such a heavy immune system. Some people already have a great one, but others have to work at it.

How It Works:

Your immune system is a natural defense of your body, and it's an entire network of cells, organs and tissues that try to fight against invaders. This includes fungus, bacteria, viruses, and parasites. They're just about everywhere. It can be in your home, backyard, or even in your office. If you have a healthy immune system, then it'll stop these invaders from entering the body and wreaking havoc, but they'll slip through if your immune system is down.

Build It Up in a Healthy Manner:

It is important that you build your immune system up in a healthy manner if you want it to last. You shouldn't rely on over the counter medication or prescription medication to always control when your immune system breaks down. There is a lot of things that you can do to help from the food you eat all the way to the supplements you take. There are even natural habits that will help you to boost your immune system, like spending a little more time in nature.

A proper diet is also going to make a large difference in the way that your immune system works. If you are eating foods that are bad for you, then they can negatively affect your immune system. Of course, if you are eating the right foods, it can positively affect your immune system. Choose a healthy lifestyle if you want your immune system boosted in the long term, which is exactly what this book is designed to help you do.

Chapter 2. Natural Supplements that Work

Natural supplements can also help you to boot your immune system quickly and easily. You'll find that it'll help to make sure that you have everything you need to keep the cold and flu away, and many people like using supplements because it's easy to take on a daily basis. Remember that you need to talk to your doctor before adding a supplement to your daily routine.

Supplement #1 Zinc

For the same reason you want to add beef into your diet, you're going to want to add zinc as well. Usually you'll need fifty milligrams a day, and it' great at keeping away infections and helping to cure them as well. Many people are zinc deficient, and you'll find that it can keep away respiratory tract infections as well. It does well when combined with vitamin C, and it can keep excessive lead levels offset in the body.

Supplement #2 Astragalus

You'll need to take one thousand milligrams daily, and it's a Chinese herb that helps to stimulate white blood cells, and it can fight off infections as well as prevent them. It doesn't work quite as quickly as vitamin D or even omega-3 fatty acids, but it will help in the long term.

Supplement #3 Selenium

For selenium, you don't need a lot. You'll just need two hundred micrograms a day, and it will also help to reduce the risk of lung, prostate, breast, and bladder cancer. It is usually recommended that you take it with vitamin E, and it can help to boost your immune system in the long run. Of course, it'll also help if you get it naturally from the foods you eat as well.

Supplement #4 Vitamin A

You'll want to try vitamin A when you're looking for an immune system boost as well. Usually ten thousand IU is recommended. It helps to prevent infections, and it increases the activity of your white blood cells. If you don't have enough vitamin A you may suffer from reoccurring infections, and you can always ask your doctor to test for it as well. You will find vitamin A on its own, but you can also find it in many multivitamins because it is good for your overall health. You can find it in your diet, so make sure that if you're taking it as a supplement, you aren't skipping vitamin A containing foods either way.

Supplement #5 Vitamin D

If you're taking vitamin D for your immune system, you're going to want to take anywhere from five thousand to ten thousand IU. It's safe for most adults but you always need to talk to your doctor. It can help prevent various disease, colds, and flus. Vitamin D has been extensively studied to help with your immune system, which helps you to prevent infections as well. Most people don't get enough vitamin D, and most people don't have enough vitamin D being made in their bodies. You can get vitamin D from the sun, but it still may not be enough. Those that have a deficiency in vitamin D already have a lowered immune system, and if you want to make sure, you can always ask your doctor to check.

Supplement #6 Vitamin C

Everyone has heard that vitamin C is great for your immune system, and you may not be eating enough vitamin C packed foods to help. So, try a vitamin C supplement. You can even get them in powdered forms to add to your drink, but a supplement on a regular basis is usually best either way. You'll need a thousand milligrams or more daily if you really want it to help, and it can help to fight off infections, including serious ones. Of course, if you get too much vitamin C it can cause a diarrhea side effect, but when you lower the dose it usually will fix itself.

Supplement #7 Echinacea

You'll need a thousand milligrams or more daily, and it'll help to prevent infections and boost your overall immune system. Of course, it shouldn't be taken for long periods of time, but you can talk to your doctor about how long you should be able to take it. Of course, many doctors do believe that taking it for long lengths of time will not hurt you. It is a controversial study, but it will help you to produce hyaluronic acid, which is an anti-inflammatory pain reliever.

Supplement #8 Colostrum

Colostrum is great if you're looking for an immune boost. It can help the growth of all body cells, and it has immune factors as well as growth factors. You'll find it's an anti-inflammatory, antibacterial and antiviral. So it's extremely helpful with infections, chronic fatigue, and even calming down an overactive immune system while boosting one that isn't working properly. It can help to stimulate your white blood cells, and it'll destroy harmful bacterial in your body.

Supplement #9 Omega-3 Fatty Acids

Omega-3 fatty acids are also great for your immune system, and four thousand milligrams daily is usually best. It can also help to prevent heart disease, and it work well with vitamin D, helping to optimize the effects of the vitamin. It can increase the activity of your white blood cells, helping to get rid of bacteria in your body. It can help with respiratory tract infections, fight off colds, and even fight off flus.

Look for Blends:

You may also want to look for immune system blends if you're looking to take a supplement to boost your immune system. It may include herbs as well as the vitamins and supplements that have been listed above. Of course, make sure to read all reviews and still ask your doctor before you decide to add in even a blended supplement into your diet. The reviews will also be necessary, and if you are asking about a supplement blend with your doctor, you'll need to have all of the ingredients so that they can check to make sure that it isn't interacting with any of your over the counter or prescription medication.

Chapter 3. Herbal Teas for a Quick Boost

Herbal teas are also able to help make sure that you can boost your immune system. You already know that green tea and black tea will help to make sure that your immune system is boosted, but there are many other teas and tea blends that can help to make sure that you're ready for cold and flu season. It'll even be able to help with your allergies. You can drink many of these teas hot or cold, as it's completely up to you. Remember not to add sugar, as it's harmful to your overall health. However, you can sweeten it with honey. Make sure it's raw and natural honey. Many honeys that are sold in grocery stores have added sugars, which are counterproductive.

Tea #1 A Flu Fighter

This tea is great for fighting the flue because you have ginger, lemon, honey, and Echinacea. When you add cayenne pepper, cinnamon, and clove you have everything you need to fight both the flu and flu symptoms. Of course, it also tastes great, which is wonderful for an herbal tea. It can even help as a mild pain killer, an anti-inflammatory, antibacterial, and it can sooth your stomach.

Ingredients:

1. 1 Bag Echinacea Tea
2. 4-5 Slices Ginger, Fresh & Thin
3. 3 Tablespoons Lemon Juice, Fresh
4. 2 ½ Tablespoons Honey, Raw
5. ½ Teaspoon Cinnamon, ground
6. ¼ Teaspoon Clove, Ground
7. 1/8 Teaspoon Cayenne Pepper, Ground

Directions:

1. Take one cup, filling it with hot water and steep your tea bag. Add the sliced ginger.
2. Add your lemon juice, spices, and honey. The tea should be cloudy when you stir it. Let sit for five minutes, then then strain if you want to remove the spices, however you can drink it as is if preferred.

Tea #2 Ginger & Lemon Honey Tea

Ginger, lemon, and honey are great at soothing your stomach, but they're also great at making sure your immune system is happy and healthy. Ginger is an anti-inflammatory, and it has antibacterial properties, just like lemon. The antioxidants in honey will also help to boost your immune system.

Ingredients:

1. 2 Tablespoons Ginger, Ground
2. 2 Teaspoons Lemon Juice, Fresh
3. 1 Teaspoon Honey, Raw

Directions:

1. Take a cup of water and boil it, adding in your ginger and lemon juice. Turn down to a simmer, and then let steep for five minutes. Take off heat, and strain out the herbs or leave as is. Add in honey, and drink.

Tea #3 Turmeric & Cinnamon Tea

Cinnamon is an anti-inflammatory as well as antibacterial, and you probably already have it in your spice cabinet. Turmeric is also known to help boost your immune system and fight off infections. It's great as a prevention method or you can use it to fight off a cold or flu that you already have. Either way, this tea is known to help.

Ingredients:

1. 2 Teaspoons Cinnamon, Powder
2. 3 Teaspoons Turmeric, Powder
3. 1 Tablespoon Honey
4. 1 Teaspoon Lemon Juice, Fresh

Directions:

1. Take hot water, letting your cinnamon and turmeric steep in it for five to seven minutes. Strain if desired.
2. Add honey and lemon juice, and then drink while still warm.

Tea #4 Thyme Tea

Thyme is also great for your immune system, and it's an easy herb to get ahold of. You'll need to have honey to sweeten it, and a little lemon juice for its antibacterial properties will always help as well. It even has the added benefit of strengthening your immune system.

Ingredients:

1. 4 Tablespoons Thyme, Dried
2. 1 Tablespoon Lemon Juice, Fresh
3. 1 ½ Teaspoons Honey, Raw

Directions:

1. Take a cup of hot water, and steep your thyme in it for four to six minutes. Strain, and then add lemon juice and honey. Drink while warm.

Tea #5 Orange & Green Tea

You already know that green tea is going to help boost your immune system, so it's a great tea base. When you add in orange zest and some juice, you're also getting some more vitamin C that's needed to keep your immune system healthy and strong as well. Add in a little honey for a sweetener, and you're good to go with this immune booster.

Ingredients:

1. 1 Teaspoon Orange Juice, Fresh
2. 1 Teaspoon Honey, Raw

3. 1 Teaspoon Orange Zest
4. 2 Tablespoons Green Tea Leaves

Directions:

1. Take hot water, letting your green tea leaves, orange juice, and zest steep for five to six minutes. Strain, and then add honey and mix. Drink while warm.

Tea #6 Basic Lemon & Green Tea

Lemon is great for your immune system problem, especially when paired with green tea. Make it a little sweeter so that you get the antioxidants you need from the honey, and you're sure to have a strong immune system in no time at all.

Ingredients:

1. 2 Tablespoons Green Tea Leaves

2. 1 Teaspoon Lemon Zest
3. ½ Teaspoon Lemon Juice, Fresh
4. 2 Teaspoons Honey, Raw

Directions:

1. Take hot water, and make sure to steep the lemon zest and green tea in it for four to six minutes.
2. Strain and mix in honey to drink while warm, or you can chill it.

Tea #7 A Powerful Cold Fighter

This is a wonderful citrus spiced cold fighter, and you'll find that it has black tea as a base. Black tea is great for your immune system, and with this immune booster you're going to have antibacterial and anti-inflammatory properties. You'll even have everything you need to kick your white blood cells right into gear.

Ingredients:

1. 2 Teaspoons Honey, Raw
2. 2 Tablespoons Black Tea Leaves
3. 1 Teaspoon Lemon Juice, Fresh
4. ½ Teaspoon Cinnamon, Ground
5. ¼ Teaspoon Turmeric, Ground
6. ¼ Teaspoon Ginger, Ground
7. 1 Teaspoon Orange Juice, Fresh

Directions:

1. Boil a cup of water, adding in your ginger, turmeric, cinnamon, black tea, orange juice, and lemon juice. Turn down to simmer for four to six minutes, and then strain after you take it off of heat.
2. Add honey and drink while warm, but some people do prefer this tea when chilled. If so, make it in advance and allow it to chill for at least one hour.

Tea #8 Black Ginger Tea

Ginger is great for your immune system, and you can have a little cinnamon hidden in there as well. You can kill off the bacteria and boost your white blood cells with the black tea that's added.

Ingredients:

1. 2 Tablespoons Black Tea Leaves

2. 5 Slices Ginger, Fresh & Thin
3. ½ Teaspoon Cinnamon
4. 1 ½ Teaspoons Honey, Raw

Directions:

1. Just take hot water, steeping your black tea leaves, ginger, and honey together. Let steep for four to six minutes, and then strain.
2. Add in honey and drink while warm.

Chapter 4. Foods to Add in That Really Work

The proper diet will really make the difference in your immune system, and you can add these foods into your meals. You should eat a variety of them on a daily basis if you want it to really work. You can build an immune boosting diet from herbs all the way to fruits and vegetables that are sure to help.

Remember that it will always help if you're making sure to eat as many raw fruits and vegetables on the list as possible. It's important that you replace your junk food with these healthy immune boosting foods. Remember to add them together when you can to create an entire immune boosting diet that works with you to keep your immune system boosted in the long run.

Helper #1 Oats & Barley

It's important to get beta-glucan if you want to boot your immune system. It's a type of fiber that is antimicrobial, and it all contains a lot of antioxidants. It's easy to add oats and barely into your daily routine. Eating oatmeal for breakfast is especially an easy way to add it into your routine to boost your immune system, and it'll even help to speed along wound healing. You're less likely to get sick if you're eating oats or barely at least once daily.

Helper #2 Garlic

Garlic is easy to get ahold of, and garlic powder will work in a pinch, but fresh garlic is always best. You can mince it and use it in your food, but some people like to eat garlic cloves all on their own. It has allicin, and this can help fight of bacteria and infections. It can help you get over a cold, and if you eat it often enough it can keep away a viral such as the cold or flu. You only need two cloves a day, and you'll find that it can be added into many of your dinner dishes.

Helper #3 Black Tea

Black tea is easy to add into your diet, and you may want to drink it two or three times daily for the best results. Of course, green tea is also great because of the antioxidants that are going to help you. This will help your immune system to start to fight viruses that may be trying to get in, and it's because of the L-theanine and the amino acid that's found in black and green tea. You can drink it iced or cold, but make it from tea bags yourself so you know exactly what you're adding into it. Don't just buy it premade.

Helper #4 Shellfish

Shellfish is a great way to boost your immune system as well. You can use lobsters, clams, crabs, and oysters. Of course, salmon, herring, and mackerel will help as well. Shellfish helps to produce cytokines in your white blood cells, which fights off viruses. Of course with the fish, you'll find that omega-3 fatty acids will be found in it, which reduce any inflammation which may be harming your body and your immune system. It can protect your lungs from respiratory infections or even a cold.

Helper #5 Beef

Beef is also great when you're trying to boost your immune system and that' because of the zinc in it. If you have a zinc deficiency, you're likely to have a lower immune system. It's a mineral that is known to bolster your immune system, and you can always ask your doctor if you are low in zinc as well. If you have enough zinc, then you have a lower risk of infection, as it's important to your white blood cells developing. This will help your body to destroy viruses and bacteria that is trying to invade your body.

Helper #6 Mushrooms

Mushrooms are great if you want a healthy immune system. It can increase your production of white blood cells as well as the activity. It makes your white blood cells more aggressive, and it can help you in fighting an infection. Shiitake, maitake, and reishi mushrooms help your immune system the most, so try to add them in as much as you can. You can add them to eggs, pasta sauce, and a lot of different stir fries or Asian inspired dishes.

Helper #7 Sweet Potatoes

For those of you who love sweet potatoes, then you're in luck because they can actually help to boost your immune system as well. Your skin is actually important to your immune system, and to be healthy it needs vitamin A, which is something that sweet potatoes can provide. It can help to protect against bacteria and viruses if your skin is healthy. Try to add them into your meals, but a baked sweet potato has some benefits as well. It's not a food you would usually eat raw, but you can put it into a variety of dishes, especially for lunch or dinner. Some people even add them into their breakfast by making hash browns out of them.

Helper #8 Yogurt

Greek yogurt is actually great because it usually has less sugars, and you should cut out sugary yogurts, as they will do more harm than good. However, yogurt as a whole is sure to help your immune system in no time at all. It's easy to add in. you can use it while cooking or just eat it on its own. Probiotics are found in yogurt, and they are a healthy bacteria that you want in your intestinal tract for the help they provide. It can help to improve your immune system, and can stimulate your white blood cells, which help to fight off any sickness.

Helper #9 Broccoli

You can eat broccoli raw, and it'll be better for you if you do. However, it is also good if you eat it in something. It can help because of the vitamin C, antioxidants, and the vitamin A, which are going to help to strengthen your immune system, and you'll get antioxidant protection as well. It can even increase glutathione levels, which will boost your immune system as well. Eating a broccoli salad is usually best, but if you can't eat it raw, try to steam it and cut out any oil or butter if possible.

Helper #10 Carrots

Carrots are also great for your immune system, and you can eat them raw or cooked. They go into a salad and a helpful smoothie extremely well. They can help to ward off seasonal colds because they are also full of beta-carotene, which is also found in sweet potatoes. When you eat the two together you are getting a powerful combination of beta-carotene.

Helper #11 Kiwi

If you're looking for a fruit that will help you to boost your immune system, then look no further because kiwi can help. It can even help your skin due to the vitamin E, but it will also help with your immune system for the same reason. It can protect against any viral as well as bacterial infections. It also has vitamin C which can help you to boost your immune system, much like oranges and other citrus fruits.

Helper #12 Spinach

Spinach salads are going to be your best friend when you're looking to boost your immune system, but you can also cook spinach if you want it to help. It just won't help as much if it's cooked. It's also loaded with vitamin E, which as stated before is going to help. It also has vitamin C, A, and K that is known to help with your immune system as well. It's vital to help with boosting your immune system that you have all the vitamins that you need.

Helper #13 Berries

This includes blackberries, blueberries, cranberries, raspberries and even strawberries. They can all help you with your immune system, and never forget mulberries which help as well. They're packed with vitamin C as well as vitamin E. you can even use acai and goji berries if you can find them, but they're a little harder to find. Blueberries and many other berries are high in antioxidants as well.

Chapter 5. Smoothie Recipes to Delight & Help

You'll find that there are many smoothie recipes out there as well that can be added into your diet to make sure that you boost your immune system in a healthy and fun manner. It's much easier to add something into your diet to help with your immune system if you actually like what you're adding. These smoothies taste great, but remember to not sweeten them with sugar, and fresh ingredients are always best. If you need to sweeten them, then try to use raw honey.

Smoothie #1 Fruity Blaster

You'll find that both strawberries and raspberries are full of antioxidants, fiber, and vitamin C. all of these things can help your body to get back on track and boost your immune system. The almonds are also great because they will help you to fight off many viruses, and it contains zinc, iron, and magnesium which contribute to making your immune system stronger. The Greek yogurt also has probiotics to help, and you're getting more vitamin C with the orange added in. The honey adds more antioxidants and a sweeter taste.

Ingredients:

1. ¾ Cup Raspberries, Frozen
2. ¾ Cup Strawberries, Frozen
3. ½ Cup Greek Yogurt, Nonfat
4. ¼ Cup Almonds, Raw
5. 2 Teaspoons Honey, Raw

6. 1 Medium Orange, Peeled & Seeded

Directions:

1. Just blend everything together to the right consistency. Add ice if needed to help thicken the smoothie.

Smoothie #2 Berry Blast

Your blueberries and strawberries have everything you need to get your immune system in action, and it can help with your skin as well. The orange juice gives you added vitamin C, but make sure it's not laden with sugar. A freshly juiced orange is always best. The probiotics from the Greek yogurt is helpful, but it also helps to thicken the smoothie, and antioxidant rich honey helps to make it a little sweeter.

Ingredients:

1. 1 Cup Blueberries, Frozen
2. 1 Cup Strawberries, Frozen
3. 1 Tablespoon Honey, Raw
4. ½ Cup Orange Juice, Fresh
5. 1 Tablespoon Greek Yogurt
6. 1 Tablespoon Oats

Directions:

1. Make sure the oats are ground first, and add the honey if necessary.
2. Add in all other ingredients, and blend until smooth.

Smoothie #3 Blueberry Filler

You'll find chia seeds and almonds are great as a source of omega-3 fatty acids, cinnamon kicks your immune system into gear and is anti-inflammatory and antibacterial, as well as getting probiotics from the almond milk. Antioxidants are found in the blueberries and honey, and you'll find that it'll help to stimulate your white blood cells as well. Of course, it has a strong blueberry taste despite the other ingredients, and the chia seeds help to make this smoothie a little more filling.

Ingredients:

1. 2 Teaspoons Chia Seeds
2. ½ Cup Ice
3. 1 ½ Teaspoons Cinnamon, Ground
4. 1 Cup Almond Milk, Unsweetened
5. 2 Tablespoons Almonds
6. 1 Cup Blueberries, Fresh
7. Teaspoon Honey, Raw

Directions:

1. Blend all ingredients together until it reaches the right consistency, and then serve.

Smoothie #4 Orange Blend

This is a smoothie that is extremely healthy for you, and it's sure to help boost your immune system. It has probiotics, vitamin D, vitamin C, vitamin A, and even vitamin B. It has antibacterial, anti-inflammatory and various antioxidants that are sure to help your immune system along the way as well.

Ingredients:

1. 2 Small Oranges, Peeled
2. ½ Cup Vanilla Greek Yogurt, Nonfat
3. ½ Lemon, Small & Peeled
4. 4 Small Carrots, Peeled & Chopped
5. 1 Inch Piece of Ginger, Peeled & Sliced Thin
6. ¼ Cup Strawberries, Fresh

Directions:

1. Blend everything together until smooth. Add ice if needed to thicken.

Smoothie #5 Green Smoothie

This smoothie may turnout green in color, but it has a tropical taste that will blow you away while still kicking your immune system into gear. This is a smoothie that is sure to give your white blood cells and upper hand in fighting off anything that can make you sick. The pineapple has calcium, and there's tons of vitamin C, and you'll find that there are many antioxidants that are going to help as well.

Ingredients:

1. Banana
2. 1 ½ Cups Ice
3. 1 ½ Cup Pineapple, Frozen
4. 1 Cup Baby Spinach, Shredded
5. ¾ Cup Greek Yogurt, Vanilla
6. 1 Cup Orange Juice, Fresh Squeezed
7. 2 Clementines, Fresh

Directions:

1. Mix everything together, and add more ice if necessary to thicken. Blend until it's smooth.

Smoothie #6 Coconut & Orange

You already know that vitamin C is important to help make sure that your immune system is working well. Other than the vitamin D, you'll find that coconut oil is also great at reducing the length of your cold or flu, and ginger is known to help with viruses throughout the ages. You'll get the full benefit of its bacteria fighting properties, and the lemons are added for the same reason. It'll even help with a sore throat. Honey is a great way to sweeten it, and yet it provides that much more antioxidants to the mix to help kick your immune system into gear. Chia seeds are great if you're feeling down, and spinach is also helpful.

Ingredients:

1. 1 Cup Orange Juice, Fresh Squeezed
2. 1 ½ Cups Coconut Milk, Sweetened
3. 3 Cups Clementines
4. 2 Teaspoons Ginger, Dried

5. 2 Lemon, Juiced
6. 2 Tablespoons Chia Seeds
7. 4 Tablespoons Honey, Raw
8. 4 Tablespoons Coconut Oil
9. 1 Cup Spinach, Packed

Directions:

1. Put it in the blender and blend until smooth. Add ice if needed.

Smoothie #7 Mango & Blueberry

This smoothie has vitamin A, C, Potassium, B6, and even vitamin K. It's great for your immune system and your overall health. The amount of antioxidants will also kick it into gear, and it has a very summer taste that you can use throughout the entire year.

Ingredients:

1. 1 Large Banana, Frozen
2. 1 Cup Blueberries, Fresh
3. 1 Cup Mango Chunks, Fresh
4. 1 Tablespoon Chia Seeds
5. 6-8 Ice Cubes

Direction:

1. Add all ingredients into a blender, and blend on high until smooth.

Smoothie #8 Vitamin C Boost

The vitamin C boost in this smoothie is both tasty and helpful to your immune system, so you'll be able to use it as much as you want.

Ingredients:

1. 1 Cup Cranberries, Frozen
2. 1 Teaspoon Vanilla Extract
3. 1 Cup Almond Milk, Sweetened

4. 4 Small Oranges, Seeded & Peeled
5. ½ Teaspoon Ginger, Powdered
6. ½ Cup Ice

Directions:

1. Mix all ingredients together, and blend until smooth.

Smoothie #9 The Turmeric Smoothie

Cinnamon and honey are going to provide you a way to get rid of inflammation and add antioxidants into your diet. You'll find that the chia seeds are great a well, and you even have probiotics in this wonderful smoothie recipe. It's sure to kick your immune system into gear, and its anti-inflammatory and antibacterial, helping you to fight off a cold or flu while also helping with any infections.

Ingredients:

1. 1 Small Banana, Peeled & Sliced
2. ½ Teaspoon Ginger, Powder
3. 1 Teaspoon Chia Seeds
4. 1 Teaspoon Maca Powder
5. 1 ½ Tablespoon Coconut Oil
6. 1 Teaspoon Turmeric Powder
7. ½ Teaspoon Cinnamon, Powder
8. ½ Cup Mango Chunks, Frozen
9. 1 Cup Coconut Milk, Sweetened
10. 1 Tablespoon Honey, Raw

Directions:

1. Just blend everything together until smooth, and then drink up. Add ice if necessary.

Smoothie #10 Green Tea Machine

Green tea, as stated before, is great if you want to boot your immune system. It's great at providing antioxidants and kicking your white blood cells into gear so that they are ready to fight off anything that might make you ill. The antioxidants from the chia seeds and honey also helps, and the lemon and orange juice will help give you the vitamin C you need, and you'll find the mango gives this green tea smoothie a fruity flavor.

Ingredients:

1. 1 Cup Green Tea, Frozen
2. 2 Tablespoons Honey, Raw
3. 1 Teaspoon Chia Seeds
4. 1 Orange, Juiced
5. 1 Teaspoon Lemon Juice
6. ½ Cup Mango Chunks, Frozen

Directions:

1. Just mix everything together and place it in the blender. Blend until smooth, and drink while chilled.

Chapter 6. Various Herbal Remedies as a Booster

There are still many natural ways that you can boost your immune system. You'll find many of these herbal remedies here, and most of them are extremely easy to use and make. Of course, you'll have to find the immune booster that works best for you.

Remedy #1 Garlic & Honey

Honey infused garlic is great for your immune system, and it's easy to make. You'll need a four ounce jar that is airtight, and it'll help you to get ready for cold and flu season. Garlic and honey are both great for your immune system, and when you use honey the garlic cloves are easier to eat because the strong taste is a little sweeter.

Ingredients:

1. 1 Head of Garlic
2. ½ Cup Honey, Raw

Directions:

1. Take the papery shell off of your garlic, and break apart the cloves. Take the flat side of a knife, no matter what knife you choose, and then press down on the cloves to help bruise them and release the juices.
2. Let the garlic sit for fifteen minutes before placing them into the jar, and then cover with honey. Screw the lid on tight. Let sit for three to six days without

opening. It should be in a cool, dark place.

3. When you need an extra boost, just eat a garlic clove and a little bit of the honey.

Remedy #2 Flaming Cider

This is an herbal remedy drink that is going to boost your immune system and kick any cold or flu that you may be feeling. Take one to two tablespoons as a preventative methods in cold and flu season, or even when you're just feeling ill. You an even fill a shot glass and just drink it straight.

Ingredients:

1. ½ Cup Ginger, Peeled & Shredded
2. ½ Cup Horseradish Root, Peeled & Shredded
3. ½ Cup Turmeric, Peeled & Shredded
4. ½ Cup White Onion, Chopped Fine

5. ¼ Cup Garlic Cloves, Minced & Crushed
6. 1/8 Cup Honey, Raw
7. ¼ Cup Apple Cider Vinegar, Raw
8. 4 Tablespoons Lemon Zest
9. 8 Teaspoons Lemon Juice, Fresh
10. 2 Jalapeno Peppers, Chopped
11. 6-8 Sprigs Rosemary, Fresh
12. 4-6 Sprigs Thyme, Fresh
13. ½ Teaspoon Black Peppercorns, Whole

Directions:

1. Take the onion, garlic, horseradish, ginger, lemon juice, lemon zest, and jalapeno. Put them in a jar that's quart size, and pack them down. The jar should be three quarters fool, and then you'll want to make sure that the roots are on top. Take the apple cider and put it over it. Roots will expand, so top it off

if necessary to make sure it's all covered and won't spoil.
2. Line your lid with wax paper, and this will keep the apple cider vinegar from corroding it. Let it sit in a dark room for three to four weeks. A month will make it even stronger.
3. Take out the cider, and then strain out the herbs. When it's ready, add in the honey and store it in the fridge.

Remedy #3 Garlic Syrup

Garlic is great for your immune system, but it's hard to get enough garlic in your system to make the difference. This isn't the case with garlic syrup. The cinnamon and honey will help with immune boosting as well. Take one half a teaspoon to a teaspoon of syrup every time that you're sick every two to three hour. Of course, you can take a teaspoon once daily as a preventive method as well.

Ingredients:

1. 3 Teaspoons Cinnamon, Ground
2. ¼ Cup Garlic, Peeled & Crushed
3. 1/8 Cup Honey, Raw

Directions:

1. Blend all ingredients together until completely smooth. It should make a syrupy paste. Add more honey as necessary.

Remedy #4 Immune Boosting Morning Shot

This is a spicy blend that is sure to help you with your immune system. It'll help to get rid of toxins in your body, help with inflammation, fight bacteria and infections, and get your white blood cells moving. Just remember that it is spicy.

Ingredients:

1. 1 Teaspoon Cayenne
2. 1 Teaspoon Turmeric, Ground
3. ½ Teaspoon Cinnamon, Ground
4. ½ Teaspoon Honey, Raw
5. 2 Stalks Celery, Diced
6. 1 Teaspoon Lemon Juice, Fresh
7. 2 Tablespoons Coconut Milk

Directions:

1. Mix everything together, and blend in the blender. Put in the fridge to store, and drink a single shot every morning.

Remedy #5 Booting Foot Rub

Essential oils can be extremely helpful when it comes to making sure that you have what you need to have a healthy immune system. With these oils you have an antiseptic, immune-stimulants, and antibacterial and anti-inflammatory properties worked into the oil that you're using, making the perfect foot rub lotion.

Ingredients:

1. 2 Tablespoons Sweet Almond Oil
2. ¼ Cup Coconut Oil, Softened
3. 6-8 Drops Lemon Essential Oil
4. 2-4 Drops Cinnamon Essential Oil
5. 2 Drops Oregano Essential Oil
6. 3 Drops Frankincense Essential Oil

Directions:

1. Mix it all together, and then use as you would any lotion when giving yourself a foot rub.

Remedy #6 A Coconut Oil Syrup

This is yet another syrup that can help to boost your immune system. Coconut oil is used because the sheer amount of antioxidants that are found in it, which help your immune system. It's also antiviral and antibacterial, while the lemon juice is also an antiviral and antibacterial. It has a powerful effect when you mix the two together, and the honey makes it a little sweeter while adding another antioxidant boost.

Ingredients:

1. 6 Tablespoons Lemon Juice, Fresh
2. ½ Cup Honey, Raw
3. 4 Tablespoons Coconut Oil

Directions:

1. Take a saucepan, and mix all ingredients together putting it over low heat. The oil should be warm, and make sure it's all mixed together to make a proper syrup.
2. Place in an airtight container, and take a spoonful every morning to help boot your immune system.

Remedy #7 Homemade Elderberry Syrup

Elderberry syrup can really save the day if you know what you're doing, and it's sure to kick your immune system into gear. It's not something you can use as a preventative, but you can use it to get rid of any nasty illness that you may have caught quickly and effectively. Elderberries are known to help boost your immune system, and it has a sweet taste to it with this syrup. They have anthocyanin, which is antioxidant boosting, vitamin B6, vitamin C, beta-carotene, and even iron. They can help to reduce cold and flu symptoms as well as help with congestion.

You can use it during cold and flu season, but you shouldn't use it all of the time. Children care usually allowed a half a teaspoon to a full teaspoon every day, but you need to talk to their doctor and yours before taking elderberry. A fully grown adult is allowed one and a half teaspoons to a tablespoon daily.

Ingredients:

1. ½ Cup Elderberries, Dried
2. 1 Cup Honey, Raw
3. 2 Cups Water
4. 2 Tablespoons Ginger, Grated
5. 1 Cinnamon Stick

Directions:

1. You'll want to put your water, elderberries, cinnamon and ginger in a pot together. Bring it to a boil over high heat.
2. Reduce it to simmer, and you should have the liquid reduced by half in forty-five minutes. Remember to stir as necessary.
3. Strain to remove your berries, and then allow the liquid to cool.
4. Stir in the honey once cooled, and put in a jar in the fridge. It should be in an airtight container. Glass is usually best.

Chapter 7. Immune Boosting Essential Oils

So long as you are getting therapeutic grade essential oils, they can help you boost your immune system as well, and they're easy to use on top of it all. You'll find that it'll help you to boost your immune system in the long run, but you can use them if you are suffering from a cold or flu as well. It'll help to make sure that you feel better throughout the year. Applying them topically, usually with a carrier oil, or using them by diffusing them is the main way to use essential oils. If you are going to ingest essential oils, remember to make sure that you have a grade of essential oil that is able to be digested.

Essential Oil #1 Peppermint

Peppermint essential oil is great for your mood, but it's also great for your immune system. It's a versatile oil, and it can even increase your mental alertness while helping with indigestion and headaches. It can detoxify you, which helps your immune system. It'll also reduce your sugar cravings, which can weaken your immune system. It's great to put in a blend or just use on its own.

Essential Oil #2 Lavender

Lavender is great at helping to support your sleep, and that's how your body restores and heals itself. If you are having issues with sleep, then your immune system will suffer. You can diffuse lavender essential oil for it to help your overall wellbeing as well as your immune system, and it can even help with PM symptoms. It also calms the body and mind too.

Essential Oil #3 Valor

Valor is an essential oil blend that you're going to want to keep if you're trying to naturally boost your immune system. It's meant to help with confidence, but it also helps you sleep. All you need to do is put a few drops on your pulse points, such as your neck, feet, or wrists. This will help you to get through the day and kick your immune system up a notch while you're at it.

Essential Oil #4 Lemon

Lemon is an easy essential oil to get ahold of, and it will detoxify your body. It can help to clear out your blood, and it's known to help with your mood as well. You can use it in a blend, or you can just diffuse it through the room. It will not help as much on its own as it will in a blend, however.

Essential Oil #5 Thieves

This is yet another essential oil blend that is sure to help boost your immune system in a great way. It has a bend of lemon, rosemary oils, eucalyptus, and even cinnamon. You can add a few drop of the food grade oil into your tea and it'll help to ward off any illness because it has antibacterial properties and supports your immune system.

Essential Oil #6 Citronella

Citronella can go into an essential oil blend that will help with your immune system, and that's because it supports skin health. Your skin is an important part of your immune system, and it's your body's first defense. Otherwise, you may get infections that can cause illness and fester. It's also uplifting, and stress can actually affect your immune system. Having an essential oil to help relieve stress is important.

Essential Oil #7 Clove

Clove essential oil is a great way to help your immune system because it's full of antioxidants. It can help to make sure that you're getting the antioxidants you need for your immune system to run properly. It also helps to encourage sleep, which is important to a healthy immune system as well.

Essential Oil #8 Grapefruit

Grapefruit essential oil is a great way to help your immune system directly, and if you're making your own blend, it's a great essential oil to have. It can be a larger portion of your blend, and it is energizing and uplifting as well. The reduction in stress through grapefruit essential oil will help to boost your immune system in the long run as well.

Essential Oil #9 Lime

Lime essential oil is known to help the immune system as well, and it can be the larger portion of a blend. Of course, you can use it on its own as well. It also supports healthy skin, which provides immune system support as well. It's a stimulating essential oil that provides mental clarity with a citrusy scent.

Essential Oil #10 Orange

Orange essential oil is great for your immune system as well, and it's a relatively cheap essential oil to buy. It's uplifting, calming, and even relaxing. With the stress reduction, mood booster, and its immune system support, you'll be happier and healthier in no time.

Chapter 8. Bonus Habits to Help

There are still many more ways that you can help to improve your immune system if you know what you're doing. A lot of it is your lifestyle, but as you've already noticed it also is your environment and what you're putting into your body. Making your immune system stronger doesn't have to be expensive, and when you work it into your daily routine, it become second nature.

Habit #1 Think Positive

You should think positive whenever you can. Stress can destroy your immune system, as it leads to anxiety and depression. If you're trying to think more positively, then you're going to help reduce the stress that you're feeling. This will keep you from dampening your immune system. When you use it along with other herbal and natural remedies, then it'll help you to keep your immune system up, and you won't have to worry about cold and flu season nearly as much.

Habit #2 Wash Your Hands

Stop the germs that could cause you illness right in their tracks by making sure to wash them off your hand. Your hands touch your nose, eyes and mouth, and that's a way to get sick. You can help to make sure that your immune system doesn't have to work so hard by making sure you aren't inviting sickness all of the time. Just make sure that your hands are clean, and you won't allow harmful bacteria and germs into your body.

Habit #3 Meditate

Meditation is a great way to help your immune system as well, and one reason is because it'll help to balance out your hormones. It'll even help to make sure that you're not stressing, and it promotes a better and healthier sleep cycle. All of these things will contribute to a healthier immune system and therefore a healthier you.

Habit #4 Drink Up

Drinking water is going to help you make sure that you're immune system is in working order. Your immune cells as well as your mucous membranes are important to your health, and they just won't work if you're dehydrated. You need to make sure that you drink enough water throughout the day if you want your immune system to keep working and stay on the right track.

Remember:

If you're already sick, no immune system booster is going to work overnight. You need to give it time. If you're adding anything you're unsure about to your daily routine, you should talk to your doctor about it to make sure that it's okay and won't interact with any over the counter or prescription medication that you have. Taking preventative methods are going to help make sure that your immune system is boosted and ready to tackle cold and flu season.

Some people will take it daily, when they're feeling down, or just during the worst of cold and flu season to give them an extra edge against what could cause them to get sick. How much you take preventative methods is up to you, and everyone's immune system is a little different. However, if you get sick easily, you probably need an immune system boost. Of course, anyone could benefit from boosting their immune system in the long run.

www.ingramcontent.com/pod-product-compliance
Lightning Source LLC
Chambersburg PA
CBHW050204130526
44591CB00034B/2082